PowerKids Readers:

My Library of Holidays

Daryl Heller

The Rosen Publishing Group's
PowerKids Press™
New York

For Caleigh, Chetham, Elliot, Hana, Harry, and Maxine

Published in 2004 by The Rosen Publishing Group, Inc.
29 East 21st Street, New York, NY 10010

First Edition

Book Design: Michael J. Caroleo

Photo Credits: Cover, pp. 5, 7, 9, 21, 22 (menorah, shamash, temple) © CORBIS; p. 13 © Dex Images, Inc./CORBIS; p. 15 © The Rosen Publishing Group; pp. 17, 22 (gimel) by Michael J. Caroleo.

Heller, Daryl
          Hanukkah / Daryl Heller.
                    p. cm. – (My library of holidays)
          Includes bibliographical references and index.
          Summary: This book explains the Jewish history
that is the background for Hanukkah and describes how
Hanukkah is celebrated.
          ISBN 1-4042-2525-0
          1. Hanukkah–Juvenile literature   [1. Hanukkah
2. Holidays]   I. Title   II. Series
          BM695.H3 H46 2004   2003-009023
          296.4'35–dc21

Manufactured in the United States of America

Contents

Long ago, a group of Jews called the Maccabees fought for their beliefs. After winning the fight they returned to their temple. They lit a lamp with a small bit of oil.

The tiny bit of oil in the temple lamp burned for eight full days. This is why Jewish people keep the holiday of Hanukkah for eight days. Today Hanukkah candles are lit on a menorah.

Many families gather during Hanukkah. Everyone sits down for a tasty meal.

Potato latkes are often served during the holiday. Latkes are shaped like pancakes and are sometimes eaten with applesauce.

11

Many families give each other gifts after the Hanukkah dinner has been eaten.

A dreidel is a top with Hebrew letters printed on it. During Hanukkah it is used to play a game.

These are the Hebrew letters that are printed on a dreidel. If you spin the dreidel and it falls on the letter gimel, you win a pile of candy, pennies, or nuts.

נ

ג

ד

שׁ

17

Many children eat candy gelt on Hanukkah. "Gelt" is a word that means "money."

Each day the *shamash* is used to light the other Hanukkah candles. The shamash is taller than the other candles.

Words to Know

applesauce

The Hebrew
letter gimel

menorah

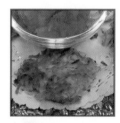

potato latkes

shamash

temple

Here are more books to read about Hanukkah:

The Festival of Lights: The Story of Hanukkah
By Maida Silverman and Carolyn S. Ewing,
illustrator

Hershel and the Hanukkah Goblins
by Eric A. Kimmel and Trina Schart Hyman,
illustrator

Due to the changing nature of Internet links,
PowerKids Press has developed an online list
of Web sites related to the subject of this
book. This site is updated regularly. Please use
this link to access the list:

www.powerkidslinks.com/mlholl/hanuk/

Index

Word Count: 197

Note to Parents, Teachers, and Librarians

PowerKids Readers are specially designed to help emergent and beginning readers build their skills in reading for information. Simple vocabulary and concepts are paired with real-life photographs or stunning, detailed images from the natural world. Readers will respond to written language by linking meaning with their own everyday experiences and observations. Sentences are short and simple, employing a basic vocabulary of sight words, as well as new words that describe objects or processes that take place in the natural world. Large type, clean design, and photographs corresponding directly to the text all help children to decipher meaning. Features such as a contents page, picture glossary, and index help children to get the most out of PowerKids Readers. They also introduce children to the basic elements of a book, which they will encounter in their future reading experiences. Lists of related books and Web sites encourage kids to explore other sources and to continue the process of learning.